The Canadian Goose

By "Martha Philbeck"
<goldenpaws@embarqmail.com>

www.homeofthegoldenpaws.com

Contents:

1.

A Story of Survival: Saga of two
Canadian Geese: Romeo and Juliet

The mother is very particular about the nest and keeping the eggs warm. In the 28 to 32 days that it takes the eggs to hatch she will seldom leave the nest. She covers

2

carefully the eggs with her soft feathers called "downs" that she pulls from her breast. These are the same feathers that are used to make down pillows, jackets or feather beds used by the pioneers.

The father or gander as he is called stands guard while the mother or goose sets on the eggs.

3.
The early morning light is casting a golden glow on the watchful gander.

He is daring me to come closer.

4.

As careful as the parents are to protect the nest sometimes it is not enough. We are not sure what, but the nest was torn apart and destroyed, the eggs were gone except for two. These two eggs are what make this story one of survival.

The two eggs were carefully lifted from among all the destruction spread around the ground. They were wrapped in a shirt to keep them warm while being transported to the house and placed in an incubator. We have to keep the temperature of the incubator at 100 degrees and we placed a small saucer with water in it for moisture. We put a date on one side of the egg so we can remember when we placed them in the incubator. We have to turn the eggs twice a day to keep the baby growing in the middle of the egg. If the eggs are not turned, they will stick to the membrane inside the eggs and become crippled. Since we had been watching the nest from the kitchen window we knew they should be hatching in about a week.

5.

Sure enough in a week we could hear a soft tapping on the inside and a soft peeping. The tapping became stronger and movement could be felt in the egg. Finally a small hole appeared.

As the chick continued to work on the hole it got bigger and bigger. They kept pecking

6.

in a circle until they could cut out a sort of lid and then lift it.

They push and push until they can force their way out of the egg.

Finally they are released from the prison of the shell. Now to rest, dry off and get stronger. They need to be in the incubator for about 24 hours to get their strength. We place a small lid with some food and a lid of water after several hours to see if they are ready to eat.

7.

It is very hard work and by the time they finally work their way out they are very tired.

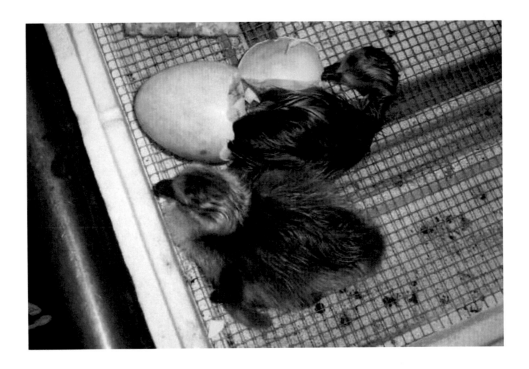

When they get strong enough to leave the incubator, we put them in a utility sink with a small lamp to keep them warm.

We let them swim in another sink. They love the water and will stick their heads under with their butts in the air. They will try to get water on their backs.

9.

They loved attention and wanted to follow us everywhere. In the evening they would sit on our chest and watch television.

They were very curious and liked to nibble on everything. They loved being held close and cuddled. When we took them outside they stayed close. They would eat out of our hand.

They would nibble on Jim's beard and it made a clicking noise. We just did not realize that clicking noise was the hair being cut until he showed up with bald patches.

10.

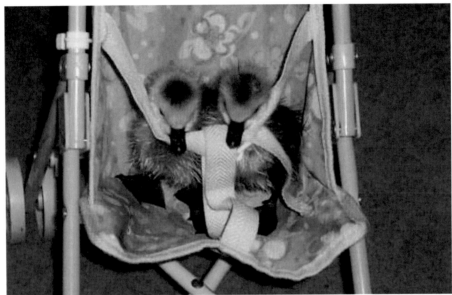

We called them Romeo & Juliet.

11.

They loved to eat grass and certain weeds.

12.

They followed us everywhere. The whole yard was their playground. They are very playful and invent new games all the time.

Soon you can see how they are growing up. They are beginning to change color and their legs are getting longer. The magic of Mother Nature and miracle of life is again at work. There is so much joy in their growing up.

13.

They have finally grown up and gotten their adult feathers. They have not learned to fly yet, so that will be the next step. Since they do not have any parents to teach them it will be up to us.

To get them to start trying to fly we would ride the 4 wheeler and they would run beside it. They finally started running so fast and with their wings outstretched that their feet would leave the ground. It took several weeks before they could actually fly. Then they got so enthusiastic that whenever they heard the 4wheeler they would fly across the pond to get to it. They also knew their names and would respond when called.

Then came "Fall" and this is the season when they travel south to warmer climate. They left with other geese that were migrating.

15.

Here is one of them flying along side while I am driving.

16.

The Next Year

I enjoy seeing the geese arrive. It means that spring is not far off. As the flocks fly in, there is fighting among the ganders. The groups of geese would come and go. Then one day came just these two geese.

They did not leave. They went to the place of the nest the previous year and acted like they were going to settle in. Before long a

17.

pile of sticks, leaves and twigs started to appear by the old stump their parents had used. Romeo and Juliet had returned.
They set up housekeeping. He would sit in the water or stand guard on the bank while she kept the eggs warm.

Finally the day came and they took the babies into the water for the first time.

18.

The mother and father keep the babies between them in a tight protective bunch.

Always keeping a watchful eye as they hide the babies in the tall grass.

Swiftly and silently they slide the babies into the water feeling threatened as I come closer.

They turn and watch.   Even the babies hiss at me; warning me not to come any closer.

21.

The babies are growing up and changing color. The parents still keep them between them for safety.

The babies are now grow-ups; they are as big as their parents. As soon as they learn to fly they will leave. We will see them next year, as they tend to return to their nesting place year after year.

Soon they will hatch and join the others. As fall approaches, they will all leave us until next year.

22.

All ready for their winter vacation down south.

23.

Another goose

Another goose has came and made a different kind of a nest out of cattails in the shallow end of the pond.

24.

More about egg hatching

HI!
Look who is here?

25.

Below is a temperature comparison chart

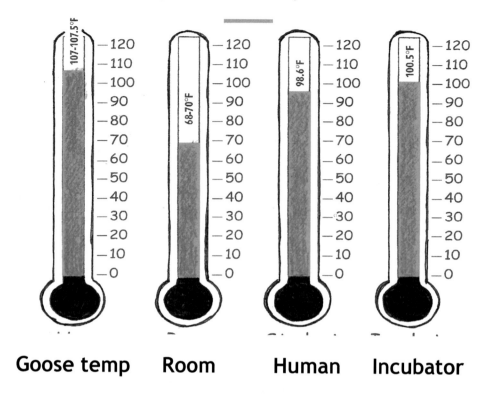

Goose temp   Room   Human   Incubator

Instructions for using an incubator

Prepare the incubator. Be sure that it's clean and sterilized. Keep it at a steady temperature of 99.5 degrees Fahrenheit and 50-55 percent relative humidity, using a hatching thermometer and a hydrometer or a wet bulb. The wet bulb conversion for this relative humidity is 81 to 83 degrees.

Step2

Ready the eggs. Use eggs that are no older than 4 days, have no cracks and are regular in size and shape. Mark one side of the eggs with the set date with a pencil or crayon.

Step3

Set the eggs. Place them in the incubator on their sides with the date side up. The temperature in the incubator will drop after you have placed the eggs. Don't adjust the temperature at this point; let it catch up as it warms the cool eggs.

Step4

Cool the eggs for 15 minutes each day and spray them with room-temperature water from day 4 to day 27.

27.

Step5

Turn the eggs at least three times daily. Additional turns may increase hatchability, but be sure that you turn the eggs an odd number of times each day so that they aren't left on the same side every night. Use the date marking to remember which eggs have been turned; they should all be face up or face down.

Step6

Stop cooling, spraying and turning the eggs on day 27, and increase the humidity in the incubator to 75 percent. The goslings are beginning to position themselves for hatching now, and turning them will confuse them. Let the baby geese hatch on their own unless they go for more than 12 hours without making any progress.

28.

Step7

Let the goslings dry and fluff for one day in the incubator before moving them.

Parts of the egg

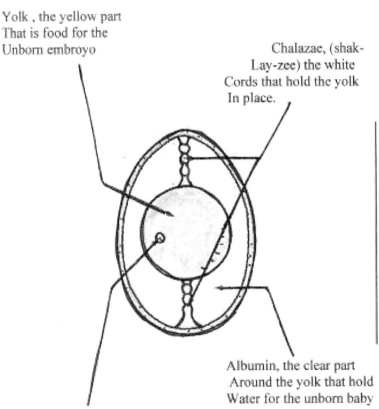

Parts of the egg

Yolk , the yellow part
That is food for the
Unborn embroyo

Chalazae, (shak-
Lay-zee) the white
Cords that hold the yolk
In place.

Albumin, the clear part
Around the yolk that hold
Water for the unborn baby

Egg cell, the white spot on the
Yolk. The baby grows from the
Egg cell.

29.

Parts of a goose egg at 10 days old

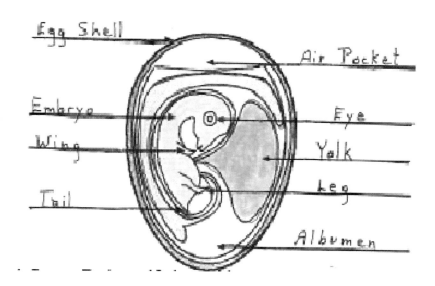

Egg Shell

Air Pocket

Embryo

Eye

Wing

Yolk

Leg

Tail

Albumen

Air cell - a space at the large end of the egg, between the inner and outer shell membranes.

Albumin- the egg white. It provides protein and water for the embryo and protects it from microorganisms.

Egg Shell – the hard protective coating of the egg. It is semi-permeable; it lets gas exchange occur, but keeps other substances from entering the egg. It is made of calcium carbonate.

Embryo - the developing gosling inside the egg.

Eye - large and prominent on the head.

Leg - one of the lower limbs of the gosling.

Tail - located at the far end (the posterior) of the embryo.

Wing - one of the upper limbs of the gosling.

Picture of how a chicken is folded up in an egg. It is very tight quarters.

31.

Yolk – the yellow part of the egg; it contains nourishment (food) for the embryo

Developing parts of the embryo

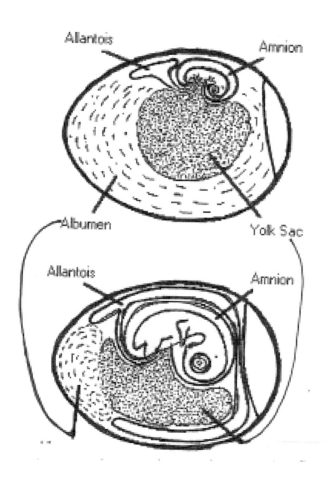

Developing parts parts of the embroyo

32.

The top picture shows the egg the first week of development. The body is starting to form on the yolk.

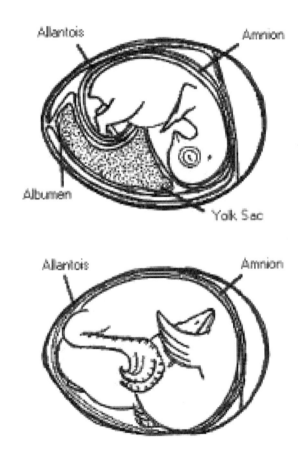

The second picture shows the egg the second week of

Development when the bird is actually taking shape. The wings, head, eyes are now visible.

The top picture shows the egg the third week of development. The whole bird is now visible.

The last picture is the fourth week just before the hatch of the little gosling. His body is completely formed; the yolk has been completely absorbed. Now is the time for listening and you should be able to hear him moving in the shell, making soft peeping noises to the mother. They will begin to peck at the shell until they break through it. They are very weak when they first hatch and cannot stand up. It takes them awhile to get their strength and be able to stand up.

The Fertile Egg and the NOT Fertile Egg

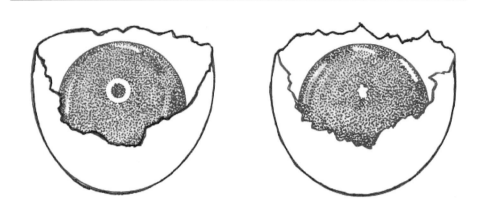

The egg on the left is fertile. The germinal disc is larger and shows that cell division has occurred which shows in the form of a doughnut. The egg on the right is not properly formed.

The Story of Egor

Egor was special. The parents had started taking the babies across the road to a neighbor's pond. I think a car hit him and broke his leg at the ankle. In nature only the fittest survive. *Mother Nature does not encourage weaklings to live and has programmed life to continue on the basis of*

"Survival of the fittest".

He was lying on the bank by the barn when first saw him. I caught him and put him in a cage and every day for 2 weeks I gave him fresh water and food. He would have died since he was unable to fend for himself. The parents abandoned him. They were gone for a week and a half. Shortly after they came back he could stand on his leg again. It did not heal properly and the foot always turned sideways and was limp. As soon as he could walk he rejoined his family. We could always tell which one he was by his limp. He came back the next year to visit.

Some more pics of these graceful birds.

"Martha Philbeck" <goldenpaws@embarqmail.com>,
www.homeofthegoldenpaws.com. You are welcome to write to me.

Made in the USA
San Bernardino, CA
02 June 2016